Do you dare dive into the pool o̶ ̶_̶_̶_̶_̶
ments and dark humors treated w̶_̶_̶_̶_̶ ̶_̶_̶_̶_̶_̶ ̶_̶_̶_̶_̶_̶ ̶ s
that cannily align "shrimp, sandwi̶_̶_̶_̶_̶, ̶_̶_̶_̶_̶_̶ ̶_̶_̶_̶ ̶ g
of life" with a confident hand? The maximalist panache of *The Mating
Calls of the Dead* takes on forbidden subjects and pulls no punches. Steve
Kistulentz's lineation, formal acuity, and soundplay give even the heavi-
est experiences a light touch on the page. "And I am waiting for the love
parade, / for the 11 o'clock news to tell me who's won, / who's lost": aren't
we all? We have all been waiting for this terrific collection.

— SANDRA BEASLEY

"I keep reminding myself // history is a list of lovers or fractures, / and
most of mine are now healed," Steve Kistulentz tells us in "It Is All Falling
Indelibly Into the Past," the opening poem of *The Mating Calls of the
Dead.* This collection beckons us to visit those ghost figures and rup-
tures, pulling out a bar stool and unraveling memory in masterful,
heartbreaking detail. Kistulentz journeys to a family's past, whether a
"moment / captured in Ektachrome" or conversation overheard and still
recalled, and into a present where mortality looms and desire surfaces
like a verse of a long-forgotten hymn. *The Mating Calls of the Dead*
charms, rivets, and devastates. Take this book to bed with you.

— MARY BIDDINGER

At their strongest, the poems in *The Mating Calls of the Dead* are among
the best recent poems of the American South. Steve Kistulentz's voice is
always clear, direct, and forceful, and though Kistulentz plunges into the
depths, he never loses his sense of where he is, nor, most importantly, his
sense of where his reader is. *The Mating Calls of the Dead* is a remarkable
collection.

— SHANE MCCRAE

There are 171,476 words in the English language, and at least 170,000 ways to avoid the truth. But luckily the poet Steve Kistulentz and *The Mating Calls of the Dead* have appeared at last, connecting us, and the dots. These dandy, searing, searching poems provide the news we need, how death doesn't care but we do, and how "no iron can stab / the heart like a poem written for a near-stranger."

—ALAN MICHAEL PARKER

In Steve Kistulentz's latest offering, "the language of the past" sings to us from old radios and across the beautiful ruins of America's oil towns. We hear the voices of the dead—near and distant, familiar and dreamlike. Kistulentz crafts uniquely sensitive, personal lyrics of love and grief, the kind that make up the textures of family, community, and region. This poetry finds its music in the shadows between buildings, in corner lots and anthracite mines, and in the springtime mud of battlefields that fill a father's memory. This work reminds us that we must look back in order to look forward, pressing through heartbreak towards a luminous "profession of faith."

—KIKI PETROSINO

THE MATING CALLS OF THE DEAD

STEVE KISTULENTZ

Black
Lawrence
Press

www. blacklawrence.com

Executive Editor: Diane Goettel
Book Design: Barbara Neely Bourgoyne

Published 2021 by Black Lawrence Press.
Printed in the United States.

CONTENTS

III.

I.

IT IS ALL FALLING INDELIBLY INTO THE PAST

My first blue car, the opened noise gate
of its quadrophonic announcements

and in the back seat, stolen Champagne
that led directly to stolen kisses

and a borrowed life, which, once I'd opened
its gift, I wanted to return. So many

objects to envy, so many abject lessons,
petite kindnesses like when the cop,

end of shift drained and tired, waved us home.
Soon my newfound program of meditation

will fall away into forgotten habit,
taking its place alongside Lincoln Logs,

the backbreak of day labor, the ritual
applications of eyeliner, steel-toe boot

and bottled-in-bond whiskey. All of that
is the past, and I keep reminding myself

history is a list of lovers or fractures,
and most of mine are now healed. Most.

I like to say retrospection is the greatest
gift, that memory drives me to stand on top

of the hollowed-out mountain of my past,
which has been strip-mined of all its meaning

by this poem and so many others, but sometimes
progress means admitting that we are driven

to repeat our great failures. My grandparents,
dirt farmers and bootleggers, mined the earth

for the black gold of anthracite coal; they dug
the same meager life from the hills of Ukraine

as they did near Hazleton. At my first Christmas,
they gave me a hymn to sing at funerals, *Eternal*

Memory, as if they knew I would be stuck looking
backwards forever, learning to read the past

as if it were a treasure map, its enormous X
a bold hieroglyph that begged me, *Dig here.*

CREED

Here, what you ought to believe
about my family: trust whatever message
comes from the mouth of a treasured dog,
especially the dog who did not trust
my father. On the high holidays
when my sister prayed, she swore blood oaths
of revenge fueled by righteous indignation.

All of us have spent decades longing
for the simpler past of undivided love
and attention, a safety net of fireplace warmth,
never succumbing to the rogue tumors of want.
Still we had our cravings, craved our having.

After all, this was the 1970s. If a creed
is a profession of right belief, then my father's
was built on a trinity of a good credit score,
serving as an usher at 10 o'clock mass,
and the immutable desire not to be liked,
but well-liked, as if he'd never read the tragedy
that spawned that curse.

                                Who for us men
and our salvation once took us
as pilgrims to the emerald waters
of Destin, where we tasked ourselves

with discovering in the languishing tide
and pearlescent sands a recipe to cure
an entire family's ills. How did I become
the only one who realized that no one needs
to know their history, as if the tainted past
I often report never happened? So here,
take this and eat it, my final profession
of the faith: only when you forget enough
of what actually happened does it become
worthy of undying belief, the lie a version
of what your family twists into truth.

WILLIAMSBURG

The tourists wanted to know if the historians made us wear
colonial dress in class, as if by making a fetish of history
we could forget we were rooted in the deep concrete of the past.
That's how the human heart works, always wanting to forget
its crimes. Before I moved on to the big time, my own crimes
were the misdemeanors of the young and bravely foolish.

The tourists wanted to know about the best place to find
shrimp, sandwiches, beer by the pitcher, the meaning of life,
as if comfort could be hand delivered to the hotel; they wanted
to know about the actor in front of the Virginia Convention
begging for liberty, and no one had the heart to say
the real story of freedom began in Richmond, an hour west.

The tourists wanted to know the name of the counter girl,
and the name of her lipstick, as if by adorning themselves
in the same soft bronzes or popsicle reds they might slow
the onslaught of time. I used to tell that same girl how
the next wind sweeping from the north would bring liberty,
when I rented such freedoms with my father's Texaco card.

The tourists wanted to know what I remembered about the woman
who brought me the telephone, a special model that delivered
only grief, its insistent tolling an announcement of my father
passing in his sleep. His sleep, my sleep, how little time any of us
found to rest, how much the millstone of grief weighed
around my neck, how surprised I was when I did not drown.

TUMORS: A GENEALOGY

I.

Everyone in my family died from it, that "C" word;
most of them grew up in the South, where
losing pieces of your body seems normal;

machine blades claim fingers if you work
a hard crop, something like peanuts or tobacco.
At the Rotary or the Kiwanis,

men who don't farm anymore wear cheap suits,
eat country ham or pulled pork on Wonder bread,
talk about Tarheels, Wolfpacks and Demon Deacons.

You listen, savoring the salted meat.
Looking them in the eye, you are hard pressed to tell
which one is glass, blinded by a glancing staple

that should have fastened a storm fence.
Gnarled fingers mash their sandwiches,
someone else gestures with the blunt half

of an arm threshed to bits
by a John Deere attachment that cost more
than your first house. Toes are just as disposable,

and someone talks about a gout-riddled leg,
a foot lost to gangrene after stepping
off the porch onto a rusted pitchfork.

What I am saying is: you expect to lose fingers
but never a breast, or a kidney
or the right lobe of your liver.

II.

When I tell you everyone died from cancer,
I'm not being entirely honest.
Cancer was the cause of their deaths;
sometimes that means something other than
cancer killed them. My grandfather,
prowling the statehouse, would say it like this:
Cancer created circumstances
that contributed to their deaths.

He didn't want to put blame on something
as tangible as a tumor, even when
they cut out a kidney, told him not to smoke,
fastened parts of his leg around his heart,
sewed those leg parts to an aortic valve
harvested from a brain-dead teenager.

III.

Great-Aunt Bernice died from breast cancer,
smoked Larks before and after radiation.

Her hair fell out with this *treatment*;
she bought herself a blonde wig

and a Thunderbird convertible,
smoked and drove fast, fishtailing along

route 12 between Greenville and the hospital,
fingers kneading the purple canyon of her scar.

IV.

At a university hospital, I held
the cold hand of my grandfather.
They removed a cancerous kidney
and transplanted a valve in his heart—

it was considered experimental.
He rose from the table,
unable to shake the delirium;
the surgeons eased away from the cutting tray,

put themselves between him and their sterile tools,
and underneath their masks,
gaped at his anesthetized beauty,
the strangeness of oncoming death.

V.

In college, I read O'Hara because he stopped drinking
and I could not. One of O'Hara's men saw death

in London, and fled all the way to Africa
to find the waiting specter in the Samarran marketplace.

My grandfather survived the teaching hospital,
the probing of earnest apprentice doctors,

the batteries and wires he joked made him bionic.
An unrelated stroke shut his mouth for good.

Still later, we buried him, the cancer cut out,
blue leg veins tunneling highways beneath his chest.

LEARNING TO SMOKE

I've written before about Aunt Bernice, but never
what happened near the end; all treatment options
exhausted, her surgeon bought her a last carton
of Larks, saying she might as well enjoy some simple
pleasures before throwing in the towel.
On my mother's side of Saturday phone calls,
hushed conversations about housework and men,
I heard only the sweep of my mother's voice growing
softer as, nearest the end of things, they talked
about the past: the smokehouse, the diner Bernice ran,
the goodness of biscuits and ham each Sunday,
how Bernice's fat brother Bill snored at home
but never while dozing through another sermon,
the farm in Blount's Creek where my mother burned
the skin off her foot in the fire of a scalding pot.

On the way to a last useless treatment, a rogue stag
couldn't outrace Bernice's new Thunderbird,
totaling the car. She told the story once,
before it became a parable without meaning.
She didn't talk about it on the phone, the same
way no one mentioned the cause of her death
as we buried her 80-pound body
deep in the hickory woods. And what of the things
my mother did not ask, like when did she find
the first lump, and why didn't she go to the doctor
right then? The questions I'd wanted to ask,
before Bernice was lost to the fog of Demerol—
did she speed up to hit that deer, was there anyone
left to call, had she seen any demonstration of God,

did she remember the 12-year-old me, stealing
her cigarettes, learning to smoke and lie
on the same afternoon, taking deep breaths
under the weeping willows of her front yard?

LETTER ON ANOTHER OCCASION

for Arline Raab (1936–1999)

Christmas Eve, the forecast 79 and sunny,
no hope for snow, your daughter and I drove

in from Miami, instead of across town. Near water,
in a rented apartment, we hatched a memory

narrow as the kitchen that required perfect choreography
to fit three cooks, each of us assigned specific duties,

so that when the day finally gave in, the table where we sat
might look the same as the table from any other year.

In those tight quarters, your daughters diced and nipped. Good cooking,
you explained, was passion, practice. The secret to the sauce—

the temperature of the butter before I set in the whisk.
We were all older, and that Christmas you were sick.

On another occasion, there might not have been leftovers,
but Christmas morning, I brought you eggs with béarnaise,

angels on toast. In bed, you shared the letters where Ted asked
your parents for your hand in marriage, though I am sure

you would have run off with him anyway. On the bed,
we talked about absent, dead brothers. And today, here, now,

I am afraid, and I cannot remember who exactly was there,
so, for these purposes, I have decided that everyone was.

THE WALKING TOUR OF BROKEN HEARTS

My father, the youngest, talking death
with his brothers, on twice-yearly visits
home, the four living brothers
yacking about how they avoided
the back break of coal mines,
the bullets of Krauts, missed everything
but high cholesterol and the body's betrayal.

And they talk more about death,
how it rises like a sniper, picking
off relatives and friends with ease,
surprise, the randomness of lightning.
They share beers you can't get
outside their corner of Pennsylvania,
voice the fear, the rattles
in the eldest's lungs, the wheezing
at the top of the stairs, the backaches,
the moral rectitude that comes
with age and wisdom.

So when they talk death, they start
with friends, the normal cancers
compared to baseballs and fruit,
the choked veins that suffocated brains
or exploded hearts. Then they move
on into the next circle, the unusual
deaths of men they knew, the return
of diseases they thought conquered,
gangrene, polio, consumption. Retirement
made them fishers of death, caught
in a wide shrimp net stretching to Florida.

Before sunset they go like pilgrims
to the family plot, and marvel over
the stupidity of the stonecutter who
chiseled the wrong year of death
under my grandfather's name, killing him
two years before Dad was born.

The others tease my father, the bastard,
until he tells of the stonecutter's gruesome death—
a man turned to a pillar of salt
by arthritis, his colon pockmarked
by polyps and tumors, his wastes collecting
in plastic bags like laboratory specimens.

They take sick joy in that, their own bodies
still functioning, capable of evacuating
the everyday poisons of their lives. There is
no mention of the aftermath, the expense,
the new roof left unfinished or the child
forced to quit college. Sometimes,
on the way home, they move on,
the cemetery just the first stop
on the walking tour of broken hearts,
and speak of the deaths on the news,
anchormen far better at talking death
than they are, relating stories—women coughing
out a last breath during the spasm of sex,
men masturbating with a plastic bag
over the mouth, the teenaged alcoholic
who mistook the low-slung headlights

of a hot-rod Oldsmobile for a pair
of motorcycles, and standing between them,
assumed he would escape untouched.

DEBT

The installment plan on which we settle
our grievances with each other, with the dead,
means we pray to an indifferent God
to forgive our debts, all us supplicants,
back broken and knees bent, hoping

for the miracle of computer mistake,
Powerball jackpot, bank error in your favor,
only to inherit a clouded mirror that reflects
your father's rounded face. I knew all of this,
as my father bore witness, and still I fell

to the succubus of consumerism, as he had,
as had all men before us. My lineage is debt,
the story of Christmas 1955, my mother
begging her parents to leave the farm,
pitch in behind the counter of Dad's store,

because the margins were too thin
for my parents to afford hired help.
This is the Eisenhower-era illusion
of post-war prosperity, my father
the civic-minded veteran, voting member

of the Rotary Club, greeting customers
from behind the counter, a Western Auto
store owned by a man who could not
change the oil. He'd sunk his life savings
into the American dream in a coal town

with no more coal, even less hope.
What hope there was could be found
in robust Christmas Club accounts, 90 days
same as cash terms. He's gambled their lives
as collateral for new stock, toy displays

flashing like nova-ing stars, model trains
puffing out their pelleted smoke, the road
to Bethlehem in HO scale, toy trucks
with the dinosaur logo of Sinclair Oil,
a boy's dream known as a Radio Flyer

wagon. Levitt, the optometrist who rents
the office upstairs, comes down after six,
taps at the frosting glass, demanding to know
when the wagons go on sale; his son
is nine, tomorrow is a bankrupt Christmas,

the wagons haven't sold and he intends
to vulture a good price. That's the moment
captured in Ektachrome, the ghost lives
of my parents a decade before me,
my father pretending at something near

happiness, the first year of his republic
of failure, of mounting debts, thinning hair;
a shopkeeper staying open late
the night before Christmas, photographic
evidence my father was an optimist once,

broom in hand, felt fedora in the other.
Next, he'll put the fedora on the glass
counter, lure his wife under the mistletoe
one final time, then tend to sweeping
the asbestos tile floors of a business

that lasted a decade more before ruin.
And there is me, watching the photo fall,
leaf-like, from a forgotten book, and still later,
writing these lines, making a poem
to be one final installment, the last payment

to settle my father's overdrawn accounts.

FOR EVERY WOMAN WHO'S MADE A FOOL OUT OF A MAN, THERE'S ONE WHO'S MADE A MAN OUT OF A FOOL

No priests walk into this bar, along with no Irishmen, and never a duck,
just two guys pretending to listen to the working-girl bartender
        who speaks only in the slant rhymes of a heavy metal jukebox.

She will be the object of an hours-long obsession since she pours
with a heavy hand and offers sympathies so rehearsed they seem animatronic.
        She's wrong for the part, far too pretty to be the one

who reminds us no matter how Herculean our efforts at change,
life usually resembles the type of narrative expressed in the elemental language
        of country music, its whimsical, whiskey-infused sorrows.

So what if the bartender and the other man in this poem
have been dead for two decades, their memories immune to the pollutants
        of yesteryear. It was a good night, with good drinks,

remembering the pretend good times we all mythologize. You can't make
old friends, but I'd rather be the bartender instead of the dumped guy, or the guy
        I was then, the loyal friend, the one who picked up the tab,

poured both of us into a cab. I'd begin with apologies, a repudiation
of earlier remarks. All the advice I gave then was wrong, wrong about desire,
        about whether laughter can be found in dog bites, shaving nicks,

fender benders, bills from well-fed lawyers who shepherd us through
divorce. Again and again we are all fools, gin-soaked and fist-bruised,
        and console ourselves with liquor but also with the knowledge

that our greatest tales will be oft told to bartenders, repeated
by our dearest friends. Anyone suddenly single again learns well
       all these paradigms of the revisionist age we called our thirties.

Maybe there's a priest after all, some sort of sacramental rites,
but more likely the change was as gradual as the graying of a beard. One night,
       in the hour of self-immolation known as midnight, the radio

no longer spoke in the language of the past. I thought of the old
joke where if you played those simple songs backwards, you got back
       the dog, the truck, the girl whose skin shone in the July sun

like cosmoline. One final warning: others will attempt to resuscitate
the spirit by offering introductions to their timorous, mousy friends,
       then give backslapping platitudes about how pain teaches us

to see the glass as half-full. Remind them how history overflows
with inevitabilities. Or tell them the honest truth; it has never been important
       to dwell on the amount in the glass because it contains

nothing you want, having been filled again and again with a vintage
you hoped never to taste. The taste of consolation must always be bitter,
       and tonight when you toast a sour memory, what passes your lips

is surely poison, a vintner's blend of memory, hemlock, and gall.

THE FINAL HOURS

Here, in a few hours, the last notes of *Auld Lang Syne*
will come drifting through the neighbor's wall.
Or maybe they will at midnight, five years from now,
when like Christ in the desert gone mad with fever,
I will be given the gift of hindsight, to see if your vision
of a bleak and ruinous future, or mine of a perfect one,

comes true. Who can tell? Maybe I knew better once
but I doubt it. Maybe I could convince you the future
must always unravel in a clean and civilized way,
until it ends up exactly where it is supposed to,
with you in my arms or not, as the kids say,
achievement unlocked. Of all the things you should know,

near the top should be this: it has been years
since I had such a feverish dream, since I felt the want
in a new pair of hands. So where does one find solace
except vodka and books? Chekhov, in his famous story,
writes about a man on vacation who spies a woman
with a small dog, another tourist in unfamiliar land.

To say what happens between them is predictable
denies the vagaries of the heart. He makes a fool
of himself, as men and fools do in the cause of love,
then the story stops. But not in my version. A man
chooses a door to open, then stretches out a hand,
to see if the woman will join him on the other side.

II.

THE ROSENSTIEL CYCLE

*Fred Rosenstiel, who spent his life planting gardens to brighten the
lives of his fellow New Yorkers, and to alleviate an abiding sadness in
his own heart, died on Tuesday at the Western Queens Community
Hospital in Astoria. He was 83 and lived recently in Astoria.*
—OBITUARY, *THE NEW YORK TIMES*, 1997

He worked Astoria, where the skyline
is cut to human height, and beauty queen dogs
grit at tetanus-laden wounds
in the rick of their paw pads,
these injuries small New York insults
of broken glass and bent needles.
No vistas left in the great flat of Queens,
the outback past Manhattan,
except Fred's eight-by-ten forgotten plots,
coveted now by someone
with connections and confidence
that the city's last orphan gardens
could turn a lively profit
as another outpost of paid parking.

Up the block, four teens, front porch grackles,
taunted Fred the gardener about his knee socks
and short sleeves, the plastic glasses,
brown paper totes filled with hand tools
and shit he carried on the subway.
Queens boys, in backwards Yankee skullcaps,
who could not know why Rosenstiel
crossed the street, how he could not

inoculate his heart against
the viral memories of Europe,
and cringed at their schoolbooks, the top one
a manual for the repetitions
of first-year German. *Arbeitsheft*–
workbook–just its hint of freedom,
tantalizing, the flash of that one word
enough to make Fred burp up his hate.

Near sundown on a Friday, the boys
shooting dozens and dice, strong
with malt liquor boldness, called Fred out,
watching the care he took to wrap his tools,
the way he forsook cab after cab, walked
past the last bus stop; the teen sergeant
asked the old gardener the question of his faith:
Slick, why are you so weird?
Fred could not answer how
he'd been conversant with the dark
since 18, since the Dutch Navy
never offered him a chance to fight.
Fred only gave up one sentence:
I have seen all the truth of the world I need;
only its truth has made me strange.

At the Old Mill Luncheonette,
Columbia students took to calling him
Professor, the way his daily routine
was to harangue, cajole, plead with them.
Rosenstiel dreamed his own master society

sprouting in New York, minions turned radical
in youth; fifty years after the war,
he still conjured a better world,
where *der Führer,* pants rended to his ankles,
could have run a gauntlet of spitting grandmothers,
or lived to stand trial. Rosenstiel, old now,
could not have had less faith in youth,
less faith in the promise of a new day–
he believed only in solid things,
things of the earth, a moistness
he could wring out in his hands.

He'd been doing this Lord's work
since summer '46, with London
still gone gray like rotting teeth,
young Fred giving a lover's attention
to wildroot and herbs, four square meters
of faith in the alley behind a youth hostel.
The idea of the place was positively Marx;
everyone should give their sweat, their noble work,
and this young Fred, avoiding the dishes,
built his supreme calluses
at the turn of a hand spade, weeding out rocks
and chunked plaster, coaxing small stalks
of beauty into the city center.
Tending the garden, turning the earth,
Fred's only close-range combat was
fighting the ruinous creep of knotweed,
his garden a large dose of bismuth
to soothe the burn of his surviving guilt.

He'd kept to it in New York,
working empty corner lots, leaving them
blooming with graces now forgotten,
little gifts his hands brought back from the dust.
It was an accident, finding this life's work.
During the corruption of his own body,
Fred kept to these mordant tasks,
even when in August the city emptied
like a bathtub; the last growing season
he worked late, searching for the sparse twin spirits
of New York summers, quiet and darkness,
to come down in late afternoon.
In the geometry of buildings—the vertical
fire ladders, the ejaculating fire hydrants
spitting straight out over the gummy asphalt—
he saw how all the right angles of Queens
dissolved into the voluptuous curves
of heat. Buses with mewling brakes
lumbered by. Maybe he hadn't
consciously learned the similar natures
of gardening and atonement,
how the hard work of both happens on one's knees.
Still Rosenstiel met his daily obligation,
dressing the juvenile growth of his plants,
each application the consecrated work
of his blistered hands, Fred anointing
each leaf and stem with minerals, manure,
his own mad chemist's pomade. Only work
could raise him up, and when he finished,
he wandered between boroughs, Fred just

the great mole of the subway, tools in hand,
shouldering up Amsterdam Avenue
between grandsons of Viet Minh and Cong
and Salvadoran grandmothers
who did piecework for the Christmas
bonus of a four-pound chicken.
Rosenstiel went to the luncheonette and
put his mind to business there
in the corner booth, over the drone
of a re-chromed Wurlitzer juke
that played the scratched 45s
of bands who were half-dead,
the old man and his one cup of coffee
just another commuter of loss
poring over the headlines,
The Daily News no truer
than Westmoreland and his body counts.

And back on Amsterdam Avenue
none of the slickee boys knew
Rosenstiel and his biggest dream:
to plant corn, perfect rows of it,
six plants per row, four rows,
on the corner across from Mattolo's
Auto Body; he thought he might be lucky
with five ears per plant; maybe
he'd yield a bushel, but he wasn't
growing for the food; the food
he'd gladly give away. No,
he wanted to grow for the harvest,

and the empty weeks after, the way fall
reduced his work to dried husks,
corpses as smooth as ancient tablets.
Planting is always a leap of faith:
you have to work hard and start early
to grow anything in New York.
You have to remember to start in June.
You have to remember how Rosenstiel cried
when summer came, a reminder
of what he was, what was taken away,
how he once had been, how all of us were then,
working on our knees in bloodless dirt.

THE MATING CALLS OF THE DEAD

begin in Germany, the muddy slog of a wet and late spring, last days of
the last just war. The Iron Men of the Metz, having stolen a town from
the Germans by hiding in the woods, waited on the banks of the Saar
River, while the nations melted around them. Engineers built pontoon
bridges and the sergeants waited to smoke; in those days, so much of
the war was waiting. Waiting and listening. The only sound the crunch
of the forest's undergrowth as the displaced persons began to emerge on
the other bank. To be a displaced person meant you were an upstanding
citizen sandwiched between the chaos of advancing armies. To be a
displaced person meant you were a peasant, another man whose family
history is a history of terror, as peasant histories often are. Another word
for peasant is victim. My father came from a long line of peasants, and
took his place alongside the other peasants of this man's Army. You could
identify the approaching peasants by their generous coating of soot and
mud. The displaced, first one, then three or five, carried a pristine flag of
surrender, a sheet somehow starched, blued, near spotless. There should
be more to say here about the displaced persons, about the gauntness
of their ribs, the one man with stomach distended enough to see the
aorta's outline emerge, a blue afterimage in someone's sunken chest. Or
the yellow eyes. The missing teeth. The ghost mouth, an opening in all
that mud. I assume that you have seen the photographs. It was a Tuesday.
The displaced came dazed out of the woods, Stalin's hellhounds nipping
at their bloodied, shoeless heels. One of them pointed to my father,
asked, are you one of us? Meaning, are you my people? Meaning, are
you from the foothills of the Carpathian mountains, the villages overrun
at the beginning of eight centuries' worth of European wars? Because if
you are one of us, surely you must know our histories. This is the question
that haunts, not knowing its meaning. Are you one of us men, fleeing
from the obvious terror? Are you one of us men, sent on our usual
urgent missions for help? Are you aware that what is left of the women
has been left behind to watch what is left of the children? Are you

aware that there is almost no one left? Are you one of us, meaning are you haunted by what we hear, the murmurations of a thousand or so refugees plus ten carts, as many horses, one mule. This is the tableau. My father, to his dying day, wondering aloud why they did not eat the horses. The army waiting for the end. A river. Beyond, a defeated army, and beyond them, the pillaging third force, pressing for Berlin. The displaced identify themselves with pride, sons of Bolsheviks and Hussars and Cossacks all. My father offered the man coffee, water, a cigarette, all of which he took. There is never greed in desperation. This was what just war looked like, refugees on all sides, emerging from the burned-out village, raising a flag of surrender once they exited the ghostwood. What did they hear? A chorus of whispers chasing them through these burned-out fields, the looted mausoleum of central Europe, the last two hundred miles marching cadence to a chorus of voices, Slovak, Slav, and Pole, swelling and dirge-like, a liturgic song. The church calls it a hymn. Eternal memory, blessed repose. My father knew this plain chant for what it was, a song to learn and sing in all its tones, a summons to worship, the mating calls of all the dead.

MULE

1.
How long the body must work.
How long the body must work until it fails.
How long the body must fail
before it dies.

2.
The father brings his body to work in the anthracite mine,
proud vista of the open pit.
The other miners, Rusnoks all,
drunk before work, during work.
But never the father.

3.
The father and his body are here for work.
He has never imagined America
as anything but
work.

4.
He has fled a land, ruinous
and rock-choked,
and he has come to America,
where the only work he can find
is exactly the work he has left behind,
the product of man and animal
plus both of their bodies.

5.
Survival is the sum total of how many hours
the body must work.

6.

After the men work,
the breaker boys bring the mule home,
so that the mule can work
after the mule has already worked,
the oppressed become the oppressor,
all our histories present in one mule.

7.

On the off days when the mule will cooperate,
the mother lets her sons—the ones
who have not yet given of their bodies,
who are not yet old enough to work—
ride the mule into town.

8.

She knows the bodies of her sons
will one day follow the body of her husband,
the father, and the body of the mule
down into the pit of the mine.
Today we call this economic necessity.

9.

But today, it is the sons who ride
the mule into town.
Among the 20 or so words
of English the mother speaks
are *be careful*, and *understand*.

10.
Understand is a rhetorical question.
You must be careful with the mule,
understand?

11.
Men from the church build a small plow.
The value is in the body of both man and mule.
The body has value.
As does the work.

12.
Because the mother expects help
from the boys, assistance
in using the body
of the mule to plow the garden.
All vegetables grown by the poor
are cash crops.

13.
When they bring the mule home
they stand on the hillside
watching the mother whip the mule
so that he will plod forward
to make the furrows in a garden
the mother plants by hand.

The garden stands on the hillside,
side lot of the coal company duplex,
where the land is worked with tools
bought from the last company store.

14.

You must never forget however
that this is the story of the mule
and the father
and the Ruthenian work ethic.

15.

At this point, the Protestants owned the mines,
and owned the product of the work,
the anthracite coal dug out of the earth by hand,
13 dollars per long ton
in the year of the father's death.

16.

Did you think he would survive?
Black lung. Influenza.
The sclerosing arteries.
It is as if you have forgotten
the economics of the era,
but we can distill them into a simple equation:
Work equals the intersection of the body
plus time. Long ton, short life.
All work of the poor is therefore piecework.

17.

Measure the pieces however you desire,
in long ton, in shirt fronts or shoe lasts,
dollar per day or pennies on the hour.
All equations yield the same result.

18.

The mother gardens to make what little they have
into enough to fuel the body.
The father possesses this wrecked body.
The unguents and liniments. Tar in his spittle.
The black handkerchief. The stoop.
A six-foot-tall man in a five-foot shaft.

19.

Each morning, the boys walk the mule back
across the street so that the body of the mule
can follow the bodies of the men
back into the mine.

Together they dig.
The product of the work is coal.
The coal goes into the bucket
and the buckets pour into the breaker.

The breaker boys pull the mule
whose bit is attached to the breaker cars
and the cars head up the shaft to the light.

20.

And then the accident.
No one can say what has happened
to the body.

21.

After, the other miners carry the father
up out of the mine and across the street,
so that the body can die in its own bed.

22.

When the body dies, there will still be
the work of the body,
work its own insatiable maw,
the body as perpetual machine.

23.

The sons have received the pittance
of their inheritance, the path their bodies
must follow. The pit mine will claim all
of their bodies; it is either the land
that claims the body,
or the work that claims the body.

24.

We leave her there, the mother, working
the afternoon of the funeral.
The boys take the mule to another family
whose bodies need more from the mule
than a widow does.

25.

The other widows bring covered plates
for the mercy meal and leave them
steaming on the kitchen table,

meant now for the strangers who must,
later that day, still work,
while the mother now
is just another baba
toiling in her garden.

26.
Some 40 years later, hurrying to fill
seed furrows on a Memorial Day,
she will fall and break her left hip.
In the hospital, surrounded by
the equally ruined, her body breathes its last.
And in that moment, she thinks not
of her husband or any of the abstractions
of light we are told we must witness
as we depart this body.

No.

Instead she pictures only the mule,
how she would sneak him the first
of the year's carrots,
kiss the broad flat expanse between
the gentle flare of his nostrils,
and whisper how much she admired
how daily, and without complaint,
each of them worked.

III.

THE UPSIDE OF SUFFERING IN THIS MANNER

Let us not forget about the scars, the self-
mortifications that we wear as garland
or shroud. Let us not forget the scars

hidden beneath the clothing, trying to burst
through muslin as if a compound fracture
tells more than one story, saying anything

other than its most profane announcement.
This is my body, blessed, wrecked, broken
for you. Let us not forget the scars of experience,

hard won, the tree rings of betrayal, grief,
and/or divorce, any combination of the three.
Let us not forget how these scars, anointed

and salved, sprout the most incredible blooms.

SOME ROSES WITH THEIR PHANTOMS

No flowers this happy dead winter, and I am afraid
to make predictions of how I will feel later this spring.
Already, in the year's first barren weeks, I am fueled
by the conviction I will feel exactly the way
I feel now—hating roses, hating the way all men do
when they learn they will not be the first to give
a woman Champagne, chocolates, or even poems.
For this sin, I will be taunted by men in Army jackets
giving roses away like government surplus, five dollars
for a dead or dying dozen. For her, I was thinking
tulips, to cover her windshield with a huge, odd number
of yellow petals, and fill the backseat with six dozen stems,
so much choking beauty she would drive to work
in January with windows down, heat and radio full blast,
her fresh face out the window like a young dog, breathing
the purity of a northwest wind that two days ago carried
the year's first snow. When I was 30, I gave stargazers
in 40-dollar bundles to a woman who should have been
the last I ever handed flowers to; now we are seeing how
that turned out, inevitably. Like the men on the corner,
I've learned to hate so many flowers, but it's the rose,
and its colorful speech, I cannot master. No flower can say
what I want. The best I can hope for is a new language,
someone inventing a code to send the message I must send,
someone whose scans are negative, whose tests do not reveal
how sick they are, who does not suffer, as I do,
from a calcified thickness of heart, a bent and broken tongue.

ON A NEW PAIR OF HANDS

I have been reading all about hands, their history and anatomy,
how the length of the span between thumb and smallest finger
ought to predict a master pianist. Scriabin surely had large hands,
demanding the suspension of each chord, playing the perfect tone,
hoping to cancel the tin ring in his own ears, the pealing he feared
would bring the apocalypse. That is how it is with musicians.
Hendrix could reach both joints of his thumb over the Stratocaster's
neck, and, tapping at the fifth fret, lob concussion bombs
at the mud-soaked audience; poets insist a lover's hands
be small and smooth, to nestle inside the poet's, fitting
together as a set of Russian dolls. Smaller than the rain,
smaller than a stray orb of yellow pollen spread
to the next flower, the finished nails show half-moons
of pink and white. Here is a case where most poets
wrongly ignore the charming gloved hands working
with a wood-handled spade in a flower box on the roof
of a five-story walkup, tending stripes of summer herbs,
six different peppers, the gloves because of last summer's
incident, an uncovered hand picking a serrano chile
then later rubbing dust out of an eye. Better still,
the garden is behind a row house, a little fortress
of hope filled with those peppers, plus tomatoes
and plenty of fresh basil. And the working hands
have two scars, one from childhood, another earned
more recently, cutting bread on a Sunday morning.
This is because I love the size of my lover's hands,
the way I imagine they once made music,
hitting an incidental, nearly perfect note of grace.

THEOSOPHY NUMBER ONE

I have seen a gun-shy hunting dog eat the eyeballs of another,
separating him from the pack, pouncing at a side angle.
Justice came minutes later, as a black bear dismembered
the dog with a swipe of his paw, just as retribution
came for the bear, gut shot by a drunken Pennsylvanian.
So much of how we live boils down to the way one day
was different from all the others, nothing mystical
or occultist about it. This is probably why so many great
philosophers failed to write anything down except
for a list of their crimes dotted with all the same vices.
Like the time I watched the end of a friend's marriage,
the quotidian disappointment of tight budgets, the inclination
to flirt or drink, one or the other's sordid past too much
to bear for either of them. Since I am speaking
in misunderstood parables, I have seen a woman
who understood how to be naked in all its meanings,
standing before me unshy, unashamed, as if the mere act
meant she offered something sacramental in nature,
and even if you are tired of the metaphors of unwrapped gifts
and love as a basic sacrament, I hope you have known
the blessings of the body and its constituent parts,
a promontory of scapula, hipbone hillocks, the subdued dales
of stomach, all of which said to me, *this is my body,*
as if I was supposed to find meaning there in the litany
of its pieces. Explain to me, puritan, why confession
is out of vogue in a nation built on shame and denial.
Now at the dawn of this post-confessional era,
I pay $9.99 a month direct-billed, just to believe
in exactly these kinds of falsehoods. Shouldn't we admit
all our sins, even the imagined ones we didn't commit?
That's what I believe. Some ecstasies are best left imagined.

Then and only then can I admit what she really said
was, *this is my body,* meaning *this is my body which is broken
for you,* and that for all the useless beauty I have
now seen, rapturous and undeserved, afterwards nothing
changed for me, wrong-hearted as ever. I will spare us all
the forced metaphors of passion misplaced, except to admit
under oath how in order to believe, I would do it again,
just to end up exactly where I started. They say employers
value men of a certain experience. One of our great philosophers,
Hendrix, demanded answers to the rhetorical question,
have you ever been experienced? So I wrote this, if it may please
the court, as my answer. As a child, I touched a hot stove
in order to believe, and later, I burned my fingers
with the cigarette lighter from my grandfather's Chrysler.
I have confessed how I often pray to be led into temptation.
I said, Have you ever been experienced? Well, I have.

EXTRAVAGANCE

So many parlor games, but that day, our only extravagance
was a luncheon of Spanish wine, its bathwater-warm undertow pulling us
        into making it an afternoon. Otherwise, a sensible tuna salad done rare,
        tartare of cold pink. Her confession: the last time she cooked,
she was drunk, inattentive, felt the nearly raw fish staring back in accusation.
I know this feeling, as I've been baited here myself, an invitation
        promising easy celebration, but the truth is we are here to grieve,
all the sicknesses and bathroom infidelities, every electric truth we've ever denied.
It's just lunch, she argued, told me how her own cooking made her sick,
        cost her husband two days of work, how crouched over the toilet,
she took the sounds of his retching as symbol, everything she wasn't as a wife.
It's just fish, I said, between absent touches of her hands. But the truth is,
        by then I wasn't listening. I was deciding what parts I would save
for next time, some listless night when we'll shuffle together at her front step,
        when we won't count our drinks, when in careless fear, we'll stay out too late,
        avoiding what faces us, the hardest truths, our empty beds.

SYMPTOMS OF LATE CAPITALISM

I am taking the unusual step of writing to the search committee,
so much verbiage about the false coinage of mortgages
plus subordinated consumer debt. Our city depends
on the microbusiness now, barbers and cutthroat grocers,
wherein the bakers, robust on rations of hydrolyzed proteins
and complex carbs, grind their knuckles into meal, raise
mountainous loaves from a starter of their first child's cord blood.

In the new fairy tales, the mirror tells us how sick we are,
though I know a few wives who are still among the fairest,
living proof of the deceit we find in the most polished
appearance. White cells, T-cells, motivation all suffer,
the blood work tells us how each is at a historic low.

Despite the transplants, we still suffer from a wholeness
of the marrow. A song from our past says, *We are hope
despite the times,* and the true tragedy is how we used
to believe those lies, fervently, how we prayed to gods
both real and false using the same litanies, *ask your doctor
if Elavil is right for you.* Or Klonopin. Dealer's choice.

The prosecutors objected, as the questions had been asked
and answered three times before dawn. We had no idea
how to end this death march, this spiral of self-fulfilling
prophecy. When the generals gave the order to burn it
to the ground, the last residents of Chimneyville
raised an army, gathered up their pitchforks,
watching as others did the hard work of rioting in the streets.

A SMALL WAR HAS ENDED

And I am waiting for the love parade,
for the 11 o'clock news to tell me who's won,
who's lost. The morning papers will promise
peace in our time, again, which the radio
will answer with white smoke, the perpetual logic
of static and denial. The editorial says a girl needs
a gun these days on account of her resonant memories.
Tomorrow, let us inaugurate our next affair
with the thunderous gallop of kettle drums.
On the evening news, we've got film in from Saigon,
Tegucigalpa, Ankara, Bilikent, Tikram, Kumadi,
Moscow, Cincinnati, New Orleans and Watts,
soldiers burning cities and towns as soldiers do,
and I drink just enough to be able to sue for peace.
This marks the end of our broadcast day.
The forecast tomorrow is for riots outside
the blind pig, burning Liberty City, Fort Wayne,
Newark, and your nation's capital. Glass bottles
of gasoline are two for one until 7 p.m.
A woman who will never be my wife
recites the terms of my surrender
from her perch on the davenport:
you be me for a while, and I'll be you.

ACT OF CONTRITION

I have now constructed a life, a fiction
to forget the unimportant specifics,
except those I could not: she was 45,
hair lacquered upright, in the manner of the times,
that abyss known as the seventies.
At the bar cart, the sullen husband,
watching his subordinate desires
dissolve in solution. Surprised to find
himself here, having spent the decade
in the familiar manner of most husbands
of the era, present and accounted for,
far too polite to show the depths of his rage.
The living room baritone in the floral shirt?
The priest who gave First Holy Communion
to both her children. In the secret heart
of our own crimes, we never imagine ourselves
convicted by circumstance, the flowers
and inexplicable bruises, even
the peal of rocks against leaded crystal.
The wife and the priest danced to a song
called "Everybody Plays the Fool." Sometimes.
I often say history could be reduced
to a list of lovers, but in this case
it was a palimpsest of disappointments
large and small, and if this is a story
I am supposed to insert myself into,
let it be clumsy, like this: this was my family.

THE LID

This box isn't Pandora's, more a wardrobe packed
with the complex secrets of time, our era of pretend
forgetfulness. You forget me, as I forget you, but not
before we admit how it felt like a moment's resurrection,
maybe more than that. I have been dead for so long,
I have forgotten. When the clouds come, I will go
to the top of the hill, bray your name into the cyclonic wind
and wait through these tempests, through every named storm
of the season, each cloudburst charged with the lightning
that, at least for the two of us, never managed to strike.

A HISTORY OF BRIEF COMPLICATIONS

A few years ago, the insomniac me watched
a movie with the unironic title *I Am Trying
To Break Your Heart*. Those bold confessions
always appeal to me, inclined as I am
to ever more fanciful ways of thinking,
as if I'm on every channel of your television.
A friend of mine is actually in that movie,
the last good thing he did before he died,
and there is no romance in telling you his story,
other than sometimes I need to be scared
all over again so I might remember why it is
I chose to live. My motives have always been
this obvious, so much so I wonder how well
you have already seen through me, whether
you know how I want to unzip myself,
scare you off, make sure you see the ugliness
first, so your decision can be as honest as I can't be.
I told you I wanted to know everything
and I am sure you know I meant it; I want you
to unveil the truth to me like the sacrament it is,
or the commandments I think of breaking daily.
Self-knowledge is a perpetual machine,
powered in my case by loathing and doubt
but also certainty, the knowledge there could be
something spectacular ahead. The only question
is whether it is a car crash or a sunset or a memory,
a pressed, dried flower left in a favorite book,
some artifact to help explain why you knew
this was such a bad idea and craved it anyway.

THE EXECUTIVE CORRIDOR

Last night I watched a made-for-television event
unfold without commercial interruption, Jason Robards
putting down the bottle long enough to be a doctor

who wanders home one last time through Nowheresville,
Kansas, the day after the missiles went flying, Hallelujah.
That was the praise song we were taught to sing,

because what else were we going to find in technology
besides deliverance and salvation in equal measure,
selling us appliances we didn't need the same way

they'd sold us the war itself. So when I heat up
dinner tonight in the office Radar Range, and gulp
it down with powdered orange drink or the one beer

to have when you're having more than one, I'll look
to the cubicle to my right, the men's room to my left
and see nothing but premonitions of the corporate wars.

Some sage told me they'll be fighting in the streets
but it isn't true. It's pretty to think so, this revolution
gavel-to-gavel on all three networks. We had that chance,

traded it in for a chance at the Showcase Showdown.
Now what's left? Christmas bonuses, stock options
that never vest. Executives on the 51st floor are here

to oversee the restructuring, the right-sizing.
After I'm fired, they tell me I'll have use of an office
for two months and that Jeannie in Human Resources

will serve as my re-entry consultant. And I tell them the most punk rock thing I know; I don't need help to know what happens on re-entry. We burn up.

A LAUNDRY LIST OF TINY GOODBYES

Maybe all of us are bullied by the past,
the protean disappointments of those who left,
those who stayed, even those who came back,

fools to their folly. I've come back a few times,
from walkabout, sabbatical, and more than once,
from near death. Now that I want so badly to find

a new life, all I carry weighs me down. I've moved
pictures of the dead, dour portraits of the people
I wished had loved me, or loved me more, from house

to house. I have learned to sit at the head of a table
that has no other guests, and imagine my regrets
sitting across from me. Recent developments started

as thrilling, but trend toward disappointment now.
This table, where I'd imagined I would once feed you
the most intricate meal I could conjure, sits empty.

Why has always been my favorite question.
As in, why do I know the names for the feminine
curve of so many kinds of table legs, Queen Anne

to cabriole to Marlborough, all on the kind of table
I never wanted to own? This last year, purging
has been all the rage, a more civilized way

of self-improvement than soaking your life
in five gallons of unleaded gas. So instead

of the massive cleansing fire, I am putting
my past on Craigslist, no reasonable offer
refused, before I settle into my insomnia

and turn on the news, watching the world
make fiction out of the absolute truth,
our new national pastime. The longest relationships

are cyclical. First I burned, then you did, and only
the high holidays find us both on fire at the same
instant. Lately I have been obsessed with obsession,

and penance, and understanding, all these things
I've gained and lost, as if love is a child's marble
rattling forgotten in a junk drawer. Maybe it is.

Maybe the idea that someone could love me
is as much a fiction as the books I've written,
or the extravagant lies told by the younger me.

This is my punishment, in the manner of the gods,
for wanting the extraordinary life. You remind me
how the ordinary life can be lovely, shame me

for putting these longings down as permanent.
in hopes that whatever gift that commemorates
the occasion won't turn out to be an album filled

with a laundry list of the smallest goodbyes.
Is that what is happening here, me destined
to spend a week, a month, alone at that table

I hate, the ritual of a thousand small apologies,
one for each goodbye, one for what is coming,
a storm without thunder, a torrent of rain

that swamps us under, never managing to break?

THE GOOD BOY

The first morning on this new planet
where you left me started with coffee, black,
followed by a meaningless romp
with a dog who knows nothing of heartbreak.

How I envy his single-minded pursuit
of the ball, the snack, the approving scratch
a good boy earns doing good boy things.
Later, perhaps, you will read my words,

these and others, and in that way, I will be
on your mind or in your bed. Perhaps.
Or maybe you've already thrown away
our secrets, driven by the same need

that makes me want to stand under your window,
follow you down the highway, make
a last stand, a profession of faith,
finally declare that one word I never said.

AN EXPLICATION OF THE POEM I HAVE YET TO WRITE

If I have anyone to thank for this solitary business, I cannot think of them now,
    nor honor them here, except to say that those who deserve honor often
    least desire it, and we ought not to trust those so blatant in their desires.

This seems to me as good a philosophy as any for choosing side dishes, the color
    of house paint, presidential candidates.

The word *apocatastasis* appears in more poems than it should, including this one;
    here I use it in the literal sense, meaning the process of being returned
    to a spiritual state of unity with God.

Olmstead Oldsmobile, the car dealer that will appear in stanza two, was
    an actual location, on Wilson Boulevard just east of what is now
    the Clarendon Metro Station. In the days leading up to its demise,
    an enterprising salesman sold hot dogs and beer in the parking lot,
    until he was arrested on food safety and alcohol-related traffic violations.

The "I" of the poem—though it shares certain identifiable characteristics with me—
    should never be construed as me. It is a far more reliable version of myself,
    filled with excuses and justifications, a complex web of lies somehow easily
    remembered.

In logic, an argument is VALID if and only if it is necessary that *if* all its premises
    are true, its conclusion is true. If one component of the argument is false,
    the entire argument remains false. I am grateful to Colin Allen and Michael
    Hand of the Massachusetts Institute of Technology for permission to quote
    from their work.

I attempted in this work to convey my disdain for the following institutions:
    the Republican Party; Outback Steakhouse; car dealers that charge more
    than $100 for routine scheduled maintenance; financial advisors who put

you into class C shares of a mutual fund, meaning that if you dispose
of them within a year, regardless of tax consequences, you will incur
a substantial sales charge; the Catholic Church.

The most certain way to get me to do something is to tell me the various reasons
I should not and cannot.

I'VE SEEN ALL GOOD PEOPLE

Just yesterday I read of a home invasion gone awry:
the proverbial lone gunman accosting party guests
as they enjoyed $100 bottles of wine,
the literal fruits of their labors. How well conditioned
we are to picture the worst in cartoonish violence,
television's routine cadence of gunfire, operatic screams.
Not here. Instead this robber left with the glorious
bounty of nothing. The hostess offered him a hug
and a glass of Yquem, served in a crystal goblet
the police later found behind a reeking dumpster,
unbroken. Suppose this criminal broke into your party,
and took nothing, not even the offered wine,
saying what the robber I'd read about actually said,
You are all good people, a bigger indictment
than anything else he could say. He'd say this, too,
You are all good people, as the arresting officers
from the first district put their hands over his head—
a benediction, a blessing, the laying on of hands—
before shuffling him into a police cruiser and off
to jail. We *are* all good people, the partygoers thought,
because who doesn't crave an affirmation,
and we'd nod, and think, *We are all good people,*
meaning only the people who are just like us.
We are all good people who desire only to connect,
and the explanation is how we convince ourselves
of our innocence. Or our guilt. The tide that washes
over us can stain like iodine, and, no iron can stab
the heart like a poem written for a near-stranger.
We are all good people, even the old masters
who got it utterly wrong: the easiest way

to remove a band-aid is to pick at it constantly,
or to leave it until the adhesive gums up
the fine hairs that line a battered heart. The rain
has the smallest hands imaginable; Mister Death
has blue eyes in only one film; the light of certain lakesides
in the south of France is exactly like the glow of the shrimp dock
in Louisiana on a March evening when dinner is cheese
and a Dixie longneck. Staring off into the valley is best
done alone; the surgeon who removes a diseased organ
is sorely tempted, after the biopsy, to put it back.

SHUTTLE DIPLOMACY

In the last spring of the technotronic era, soldiers on the quad
practiced disobeying direct orders while ambitious Henry polished
his dissertation, a how-to primer on world domination,
ignoring the approved prospectus on large conscious American persons.

Memoranda extant from the Department of Inhumanities ridiculed
young Kissinger's early work as pastiche, constructed from newspaper
clippings, redacted Freedom of Information Act requests,
gelatinous recipes from the Endless War Department no one thought to try.

The sound of soldiers marching through the Mekong is the squish,
onomatopoetic, of wingtips sodden with the blood of the conscripted,
and his wanderings, a life seen as a road movie without sidekick
or comic relief: Damascus to Jerusalem, Paris to Peking

(as it was called before the rebranding) back to New York,
where the park's burning bushes spoke the incontrovertible truths
of easily digestible dialectics: tastes great versus less filling,
unconditional surrender versus an honorable peace, the sin

for which he must atone. The sentence from the tribunal:
Henry chisels the names of the dead into his black granite countertops,
those slain for the false witness he had borne, and each morning
the slate is wiped clean. His sleep is nothing but nightmares

wherein young lions become old, lose their teeth, before he wakes
to the taunts of Amazonian blonds who ask, what use is power
when no lioness will submit to it? On the road to Jerusalem,
he picks up a rock, forced at gunpoint to retrace his steps.

THE UPSIDE OF SUFFERING IN THIS MANNER (REPRISE)

Let us not forget about the scars, the self-
mortifications we still wear as garland
or shroud. Equally let us not forget the scars
hidden beneath our clothing, trying to burst
through muslin as if a compound fracture
told more than one story, saying anything
other than its most profane announcement.
Let us not forget the stories, how the scars—
raised on a diet of beatings and white bread—
grew like a fungus when fed the proper amount
of the cheapest possible liquor.

Let us not forget the songs about the scars,
or how those who know nothing of ritual
scarification think they are listening to love
songs, as if the people who commanded us
to *wear our love like heaven* or taste *lips
like sugar* weren't talking about the same kind
of cutting, of torture. That's why I listen
only to the great hits of yesterday and today,
songs to learn and sing that tell the truest story,
how I have suffered here, and there. Give me
your hand, slide a most wicked finger over
my wounds, the only thing that proves I believe.

THE COURAGE TO BUILD

I would like to think we require forgiveness,
mine and yours, or yours and his, the remission
of sins we have been seeking since the blue
teenaged moments when you and I, half a country
apart, stumbled into those first moments
of recognition; we were different and about
to change. But this is about how much now
we are alike, the ways in which one day we might
be fused together. Let the changes come again
in torrents like spring rain and ready me to emerge
from all of this as someone newer, and better.
Since you are older, I suppose I ought to ask
your permission here, or confess my sins,
that Wednesday I stood at the causeway's edge,
between the machine-planted palms and breakwater,
looking through the burn of morning fog trying
to decipher which of 100 planes
might be the method of your departure and escape.
You told me from the start you were a runner
and I was stubborn enough to think that
to tell a woman you love her would be enough.
And then, I never said it, until here, clumsy
and unrhymed, oafish in its bluntness,
like the assessment that I'm broken, that I've needed
fixing once and again, that I need to reach
out and ask for someone to heal me. Yes, there is
a want, and a need. And maybe in both of us,
a lack of courage, too, one that means we work
separately for now, and perhaps later we can
mortar a life together. It's human to say someone

was always going to be disappointed,
and the Vegas oddsmakers have made me
the favorite here, as if they knew I would end up
suffering some kind of permanent confusion,
as if someone dropped me on a corner in Goochland,
Virginia at 3:30 A.M. without a good map, a phone,
or money for coffee. Since this is becoming post-
confessional, I have already told how every time
I have tried to build something, it has ended badly,
the result suggesting, like ammonia and chlorine,
whatever I was forcing together should never
have been combined in the first place. Sometimes
though, we need catastrophe, we need to blow up
the workshop, and let others sift for the answers
like fossils found in the valuable rubble. Failure
must always be built on small successes, the same way
hints of destruction come from heavy water experiments.
So this is both praise song and admonition, a way
of asking, too. You and I were taught how
the greatest reward comes from the greatest risk.
What you are building now equals progress,
forward movement requires courage, and don't
we have to continue? Almost every song
we both have ever loved is about knowing this,
the inevitable forward march of time. Like the song
says, *every little thing is gonna be all right.*
And I cannot help but think about all we have
not done, the songs we have not danced to,
the insidious ones where your hips pushed
from side to side and the shake of your head

moved stripes of hair across your forehead,
the way you might have thought to pull me close.
I can hear those songs, and every one is about girls
and cars and money, sure, but also love and courage,
meaning the faith to sometimes fail. Or disappoint.
Sure, things will always change—sometimes
that means you get a butterfly from the carcass
of a dead insect, instead of divorce. You have heard
much about my earlier life, which is over now. Faith
equals love equals courage, and what I would not give
if someone could grant me more of all three.
What can I possibly say about the ongoing argument
between heart and head, how I know—whether
one night or the *thousand rainy days since we first met*
—everything that feels inevitable must happen
according to someone else's sense of time.

THE LIFE DOMESTIC

A grant from Monsanto sponsored this program of violence, or Dow,
or General Dynamics, I've forgotten, so much evaporated history.
It was scheduled to open with the traditional Bicentennial minutes
of invocation. No one wanted to admit how prayer could be seen
as the mumblings of the dispossessed, an epidemic of dyskinesia
the priciest meds could no longer suppress. There can be nothing
humble about a modern supplicant if circumstance leaves you begging
for surplus cheese. These days, we've turned away from the television,
as no one has to tell us what goes on in our best bedroom communities.
We're guilty, self-convicted, the road to a stranger's bed paved
with the skulls of priests. Someone makes sandwiches of broken glass
and light mayonnaise for the children of the divorced, who are us.
Then at the children's mass, the congregation pins a heretic to the altar
and sells him insurance, and no one has come to the folk mass since 1974.
The priest waxes his chest, another mortification of modern flesh.
A temporary injunction commands us: speak of love only as metaphor,
a blood diamond as rare as that Indian guy whose fingernails stared
out at us from the inside cover of *The Guinness Book*. We bake
bread and drink wine in remembrance of first kisses; we preen
for possible mates until we lure them upon the rocks. Our ovens
make bricks out of other bricks, mortar from spittle and clay.
Each Monday morning, we bear false witness against our neighbors
and covet their wives, contaminate their drinking water with semen,
I mean fluoride. By statute, kisses remain theoretical, or else limited
to cars and hotel bars. Fire needs fuel, accelerant, ignition. So I ask,
do this in memory of me. I am fire. The house in its natural state
is empty and burns. Bird songs lull us to sleep and the night owl asks
only, *what?* You have never needed examples to prove we are inevitable,
so why start now? Come to me, I tell you, and I will protect you.

THE HIGH MASS

Sometimes I like to imagine a religion made of nothingness,
all the pageantry and ritual devoted to the truth as we find it,
the disappointments of high school through middle age,
love letters unsent or returned unopened. In that cathedral,
I could pledge a tithe of bourbon. In the same manner,
my hope is finite, running out like sands through the hourglass,
except mine is more like a fuel gauge blinking on the dash
of a 40-year-old sedan, warning me of the immediate need
to remake and remodel. Of course, if this were true,
I would have run out years ago, the victim of poor planning,
of my usual emotional greed, a lifetime of carelessness,
of never watching for warning signs. Or maybe I speed through
them. I've certainly been accused of that before. Even today,
when I mow my lawn, dodging the bees, I step over key limes,
rotten and riddled with sugar ants. The blade finds them,
spits them out sideways, and as the fragrance wafts up,
a pledge of summer, or a hint of its near end, I know
my entire life can be found here in the smell of cut grass,
of wild onion and strawberry fighting through the hydroseeded
carpet of the past. This is the story of 400 Saturdays,
where I can still smell the low quality burn of my father's
dime store El Producto as he hosed off the driveway,
ran a sponge over the Oldsmobile, summoned his best friend
with the crack of a beer can, that fresh spring of carbonated glory
that wafted over the fine middle Americans enjoying the one beer
to have when they were having more than one. After dinner,
we'd retreat and together rub the high spit shine of success
into our wingtips, a Saturday night ritual he'd learned in basic
training, as if success came with a lifetime supply of Kiwi polish,
gun oil and Brasso. What else is the city at 4 A.M. but the dreams

of a thousand dead fathers still in the basement polishing shoes,
happiest in the bygone era of cream-top milk bottles
and day-old bread for a nickel. Sometimes I like to imagine
how my first holy communion was a kind of hallucinatory
Bromo Seltzer, the wandering specters of the dead, alive
and busy, streaming out of the stone church on Gallatin Street,
where the priest sported yet another panda eye from a night
of cruising the Maine Avenue waterfront, a church where
the men waited between marriages, between wars. Sometimes
I like to forget that I imagined a life without the church,
the ritual of the lawn, the VFW with Uncle Mike, the shoes,
the candles, the extra few minutes of the high mass, stretching
out the only hour each week when that dashboard gauge of hope
flashed its angriest red, reminding me to hit my knees, pray to forget.

VALEDICTORY ON LEAVING THE MEADOWS OF ASPHODEL

I have spent years apologizing to the dead,
telling them the ways in which their being dead
was the greatest of my recent disappointments.
I have spent years, too, being a disappointment,
so much so that if the dead were to return,
I would be shunned by the dead, unforgiven.
I have spent years waiting for the voices
of the dead to stop inviting me to join them.
After that year when there was so much silence,
I spent still more of the following years
asking why that midnight choir of angels
went quiet, what part of soaring harmony
had I disturbed with my persistent questions,
my selfish desires. I spent the following years
immersed in the study of my daughter's face,
only to find it made of the constituent parts
of all my beloved dead. I then spent years
avoiding the obvious advice of the same dead,
preferring the frivolous pursuit of answers
man is not meant to have. I spent those years
borrowing against the future, a mortgage of spirit.
I have spent years waiting for the answers
to be revealed, the clay to be washed from my eyes.
As the story says, only those with ears shall hear.
Today, that ends, and I lift my blind eyes
to the vague intimations of light promised
by the future, and I will spend no more time
mourning a past I cannot understand,
the dead who never once bothered to answer.

SALVATION IS ALWAYS AWKWARD TRAVEL

I am tethered to the same nothingness
found in the bottom of that dank place
the authorities describe when they demand
to get to the bottom of things. I got there once,
the bottom I mean, a surprisingly nice
neighborhood of manicured hair and nails
fit for any crucifixion. At night, I rolled up
my pallet and walked, and again in daylight.
I found hints of our destruction in heavy water
experiments. I covered your windshield
with the propaganda of daisies. Who is this *you*
I keep referring to? Look in the mirror.
Kiss her on the mouth. Redraw her mouth
the way you might gerrymander anything
your heart and loins tell you to crave,
tell you to steal. In that bad neighborhood,
a woman owned a dog who kissed the mailman
on the mouth and bit the children. She called
him Prole, and that dog was decidedly our people.
She taught him to bark a Hallelujah chorus,
in such a clarified tenor you didn't even notice
his three heads. So the demon dog sang
his own harmonies, guarding the underworld
where I once hoped to make a peasant homestead.
I wish I could tell you how I lowered myself
into the first ripple of the healing waters there,
but instead I left, rising up towards a future
where I kissed you on the mouth and told you
even the invented parts of this hold true.

ACKNOWLEDGMENTS

I wish to thank the following editors and journals for publishing these poems, some in earlier versions:

"It Is All Falling Indelibly Into the Past" and "Theosophy Number One" appeared in *Another Chicago Magazine*. "It Is All Falling . . ." takes its title from a line from Don DeLillo's novel *Underworld*.

"Williamsburg," "For Every Woman Who's Made a Fool Out of a Man, There's One Who's Made a Man Out of a Fool," and "A Laundry List of Tiny Goodbyes" appeared in *Miracle Monocle*.

"Act of Contrition" appeared in *Gettysburg Review*.

"Tumors: A Genealogy" originally titled "Malignancy," appeared in *Southern Humanities Review*.

"Learning to Smoke" and "On a New Pair of Hands" appeared in *New Letters*.

"The Walking Tour of Broken Hearts" appeared under the title "My Father, Talking Death" in *Paterson Literary Review*. Its title is taken from a song by Luis Bango.

"The Final Hours" appeared in *Phi Kappa Phi Forum*.

"The Rosenstiel Cycle" appeared in *Quarterly West*, and was awarded the Writers at Work Fellowship in Poetry.

"The Mating Calls of the Dead" and "The Life Domestic" appeared in *The Common*.

"The Upside of Suffering in this Manner," "Extravagance," and "The Upside of Suffering in this Manner (Reprise)" appeared in *A Poetry Congeries*.

"Letter on Another Occasion" and "Some Roses with Their Phantoms" (under the title "Against Roses") appeared in *Crab Orchard Review*. "Some Roses . . ." takes its title from a painting by Dorothea Tanning.

"The Lid" appeared in *Southern Indiana Review*.

"A Small War Has Ended" appeared in *PANK*.

"I've Seen All Good People" appeared in *Pine Hills Review*.

"The Executive Corridor" appeared in the anthology *Clash by Night*, edited by Gerry Lafemina and Gregg Wilhelm. It is loosely based on the song "Koka Kola" by the Clash. It also uses a phrase, "premonitions of the corporate wars," which appears in a painting called "The Last Washington Painting", by Alan Sonneman.

"For Every Woman Who's Made a Fool Out of a Man, There's One Who's Made a Man Out of a Fool" takes its title from a song by Nick Lowe.

Occasionally these poems quote in passing a short series of words or a small phrase taken from popular music. These selections are italicized.